De rawl

CW01630876

How it is spoke

by

Peter Wright

EX LIBRIS
R. ELVINS

DALESMAN BOOKS
1975

25p.

THE DALESMAN PUBLISHING COMPANY LTD., CLAPHAM (via Lancaster), NORTH YORKSHIRE

First Published 1975

© Peter Wright, 1975

ISBN: O 85206 297 4

ACKNOWLEDGMENTS

Most grateful thanks to British Rail employees, especially Inspector Geoffrey Smith of Derby; to the staff of Sheffield University Institute of Dialect and Folklore for permission to sift through their marvellous archives of latest Derbyshire material; to my colleagues Ian Jackson and Neville Haddock; and to willing helpers the length and breadth of the county.

Printed in Great Britain by
GEO. TODD & SON,
Marlborough Street, Whitehaven.

THE DERBYSHIRE DRAWL

SOME will object to this book's title. They will want to classify it as the Derbyshire *drool* (a local word for "nonsense"), *dawdle, doggerel* or *drivel;* but if we even get outsiders to admit that it has a dialect, a fact really as plain as the nose on your face, we are making headway. Then gradually we can take up the question of the compulsory teaching of Derbyshire in all British schools and universities, leading to G.C.E. and degree examinations in the subject.

As a former Derbyshire resident, and even now living on its borders, your author tries to screen any potential immigrants in case they disfigure the speech of the county, and recommends you to do likewise. *The Derbyshire Drawl* actually completes a quartet of dialect books, following *The Lanky Twang, The Yorkshire Yammer* and *The Cheshire Chatter,* so if you must have another county we're not stopping you.

But half a million people say Derbyshire's best. It breeds fast bowlers and resilience, a rugged outlook and an honest philosophy not to be confused with the traits of namby-pamby counties. Life in Derbyshire goes on more slowly than elsewhere — not a bad thing when you consider the "instant politics" and hasty decisions of the world outside. Sadly though, many travellers barely recognise Derbyshire as they hurry north or down to London. To them it is just an area on their way to their destination. They can easily spot the outlandishness of the "Geordie", the buffoonery of the Liverpudlian or the quaintness of the Devon farmer, but not Derbyshire with its special language.

But, far from being unrecognisable, Derbyshire's talk is a fascinating mixture of both East Midland and West Midland forms, along with others that have crept in from the North. Derbyshire is justifiably proud of its great houses, moors, rivers and bridges, and should be equally renowned for its dialect. Yet all the county doesn't speak alike : that would be expecting too much. Towards the middle they say sometimes *ee* for *ay,* just as in parts of Cheshire and Staffordshire. So they use *ommer an' neels,* and on the ground they see *deezies* and *sneels.* "Do-it-yourselfers" from North Derbyshire will do a thing *thersells* (a Northern feature) while their comrades farther south do it *thersens* (North Midland).

In this connection, it is heartening to report that Derbyshire sounds are making an impact on seats of learning. A Bakewell man sent his son to Cambridge University and in the summer term went to see how he was getting on. Shown into the study of a man he took to be the headmaster, he asked was his lad all right. "Oh, ah", replied the professor.

PLACE-NAMES

RIVER NAMES throughout England are often Celtic in origin. This rule applies not only to Derbyshire's main rivers, the *Darren* ("Derwent"), Dove and Trent, but to their tributaries Amber, Dane, Goyt, Noe, Rother and Wye. Other Celtic names include the *tors* of the Peak area, Chevin, Kinder and Mellor.

Place-names show that the Anglo-Saxons reached Derbyshire rather later than many other counties, no doubt because it is in the middle of England. The cluster of Celtic names in Derbyshire's north-west corner shows that the Celts clung on there quite a while; and the lack of places with *-ingham* (like Birmingham or Nottingham) shows that the whole county was colonised rather late, when the custom of making such place-names had stopped.

Clearly, though, most names are from Old English — e.g. Mickleover from *mycel* ("great") plus *ofer* ("slope or ridge"); Matlock meaning "oak where the moot or local parliament was held"; and the many *lows* meaning "burial mounds", as in Baslow, Hucklow and the famous Arbor Low. Alfreton was "Alfred's town", Bramley was "broom pasture". The various *hopes* (Alsop, Elleshope, Glossop, Heslop, Rushup) refer to semi-circular recesses or hollows in the hills. All the examples of *worth* ("wood") in the north-west tip of Derbyshire suggest that early settlers there came up the river valleys from Cheshire.

Scandinavian influence is weaker in Derbyshire than in Nottinghamshire, Lincolnshire or Leicestershire. Nevertheless, we find *-by* and *-thorpe* meaning "settlement" as in Bretby and Derby, Hackenthorpe and Wilsthorpe; and *gate* for "way" (not the kind you unlatch) as in Derby's *Irongate* and *Sadler Gate,* Chesterfield's *Saltergate,* and *Ambergate.* Latin and French names are scarce (they are collected more easily in a southern county like Dorset). Still there is Buxton from a Roman spelling *Bucostenum;* and from French Belper ("beautiful retreat"), the innards of Alsop-en-le-Dale and Chapel-en-le-Frith *(frith - "wood"),* and probably Old French *haut* for "high" now cleverly disguised in Ault Hucknall.

Village names hint of what the countryside was like and the useful things to be found in it. Dore, another Anglo-Saxon name, really was a "door", a narrow pass through the hills which formerly separated the kingdoms of Mercia and Northumbria. Mapleton was a farm where maple trees grew and Darley a meadow famous for deer. There were ash trees at Borrowash and willow trees at Wilne, which means "willow island". Before watermills were used, it was common to have handmills or querns, which were made from a suitable stone at Quarndon ("quern-stone hill"). Water-wheels, which became the later source of power, had to have grinding troughs and grindstones to edge the tools that created Sheffield's great cutlery industry. Derbyshire millstone grit supplied many of the wheels, and here, for instance, you can see the importance of Grindleford, named from the *grindlestone* ("grindstone").

Places sprout nicknames. Youlgreave is known as *Pommy Town,* the village of Stanley is *Monkey Park,* the town of Heanor is *Tag Hill* and Brassington is *Dodge City.* Woodville is *Box* and a group of mortgaged property there is known as *Monkey Island;* whilst residents of Poolsbrook, near Chesterfield, call their abode the *Spike* and Newbold is referred to scornfully as *Soft Watter Town.* Sociologists could learn a lot from these names.

Birthplaces can foist embarrassing nicknames onto their natives. *Derby Rams* from the coat-of-arms is not too bad a name, for either Derby's citizens or its soccer fans, but *Tidza sawyeds* is more unfortunate. It arose because Tideswell people were alleged to have found one of their cows stuck with its head between the bars of a gate and decided that the only way to release it was to saw off its head. There is other alleged evidence of Tideswell stupidity. *Tidza* ducks were gobbling all the corn before the cocks and hens could reach it, so a farmer, it is claimed, cut their bills to a point to give the others a better chance. And there is the story of *Tidza* band which, late one Christmas night and well fortified by ale, became muddled in their geography and, mistaking the dim outline of a haystack for a house, struck up a carol. Noticing a steadily increasing glow of light, one musician urged, "Come on! They're getting up", but it was the moon peering over the stack.

Even without attached stories, some of Derbyshire's place-names set your thoughts flying. Most children are born in wedlock but some in Matlock. Consider the descriptiveness of the names Featherbed Moss and the Windgather Rocks, the alliteration of Chinley Churn; the danger of Devil's Dyke, Cutthroat Bridge and Muggington; the misery of Youlgreave, Unthank, Bleak House and Coldharbour Moor; the violence of Knockerdown; the appetising Puddingpie Hill; and distant-sounding places like Jericho, Gibraltar and The Heights of Abraham.

Some names are certainly misleading. *The Mountain* is only 795 feet. And *Stoney Cloud* near Ilkeston has nothing to do with the sky, its second part being from Celtic *clud* ("rock"). A local yarn tells us that this sandstone outcrop is the last mountain in the Pennine Chain. Coal Aston is another place with a deceitful name, unconnected with coal. It is from twisting the spelling of *Cold Aston,* where *Aston* meant "east settlement". It is cold because of its exposed position on its ridge : there are very few summer days when you can sit out pleasantly in a garden in Coal Aston.

Don't believe all you see on signposts : the local authorities only put them up to confuse you. If one reads "Bolsover", ignore it and search for *Bolser* or *Bowzer;* if it seems to say "Edensor", ask for *Ensor.* Here are a few more necessary corrections :

Artle — "Harthill"	*Eem* — "Eyam"
Artsun — "Hartshorne"	*Fooler* — "Foolow"
Asher — "Ashover"	*Greezly* — "Gresley"
Cawla — "Callow"	*Newbut* — "Newbold"
Dawbry — "Dalbury"	*Plessley* — "Pleasley"
Eck'nt'n — "Eckington"	*Rossan* — "Roston"

Two nearby towns are Ashbourne, locally *Ashbun;* and Wirksworth, called *Wosser, Wusser* or, worse still, *Worser.* Lying north of the general line between them are the three villages of *Brassen, Carsen* and *Tissen.* True to form the bureaucratic mind lengthens them, turning these little triplets into the mouthfuls of Brassington, Carsington and Tissington. No wonder the rates go up!

Though Derbyshire is often *Durbyshire,* few people forget that Derby is pronounced *Darby,* even though, as in *clerk,* the old and the modern spelling have *e.* The name is from a Danish settlement *Deoroby,* made at or very near a former Old English one with the very different name of *Northworthy,* this native name having later been lost.

Rosemary Meynell, contributor of so many delightful articles to *Derbyshire Life,* complains that place-names seem to have been affected by snobbery. When everybody could read, they started to get things wrong, resorting to spelling pronunciations. She was brought up to pronounce the village Idridgehay as *Ithersay,* but has had to give up the fight. Even natives of Parwich say *Par-which* and not, historically, *Parridge;* but she champions *Spoondon* for Spondon, *Uxeter* or *Uttoxeter* instead of *U-tox-eter,* and *Burrowash* instead of the hideous *Borrow-wash.* Good luck to her and all lovers of traditional place-names!

Incidentally, some well-known surnames arise from Derbyshire places. Anybody equipped with the name Allsop, Brailsford, Charlesworth, Enser, Padley, Shirley, Smalley or Tansley — to name just a few — can pride himself on coming from formidable local stock.

Finally let's explore Derbyshire cave-names, some of which are surprising. *Devil's Arse* — forgive the language — amounts to a technical term for the Peak Cavern. Cotton's Cave in Beresford Dale was where Charles Cotton hid from his creditors and Poole's Cavern at Buxton is apparently called after a 15th-century robber who used it as his retreat. *Bossen Hole* near Stoney Middleton is from an old Derbyshire name, *bauson* for a badger. And a cave in the Winnats Pass, for long years nameless, suddenly became *Suicide Cave* following a coroner's verdict. Some people, however, are never satisfied with Derbyshire's caves. The *Manchester Guardian* once quoted a disgruntled lady in a boat in Speedwell Cavern telling a friend, "I think it's dear at a shilling. Why, at Blackpool you can see gnomes as well for sixpence".

SAYINGS

DERBYSHIRE-DWELLERS naturally think their county is superior. An old saw reads, "Nottinghamshire full of hoggys/Derbyshire full of doggys" (except for food, most of us prefer the dogs). Staffordshire and its people are usually thought rather comical. Thus: " 'E's talkin' Staffordshire Irish (–nonsense)", "Water runs uphill in Staffordshire", "Staffordshire is on the back of the map".

Around Derbyshire places cluster many interesting sayings such as these:

Ashford, etc: "Ashford in the water,/Bakewell in the spice,/Sheldon in the nutwood,/and Longsden in the lice".

Barlow and Youlgreave: Of both these centres of wisdom it is said "they put t'pig on t'wall to watch t'band go by".

Baslow, etc.: "Baslow for gentlefolks,/Calver for trenchers,/Middleton for rogues and thieves,/and Eyam for pretty wenches". It is good for the plague village to have something pleasant said about it.

Derby: "Derby born, Derby bred, Strong i' th' arm and wick i' th' yed". Luckily etymologists agree that *wick* can be derived from *quic*k rather than *weak,* as jealous rivals keep suggesting.

Dore: "Dore bugs,/Water clogs,/Eating out o' swill tubs;/ Up a ladder and down a wall,/A penny loaf will serve you all" (a taunt by the lads from neighbouring Totley).

Hardwick and Kinder: ' Hardwick Hall,/More glass than wall./Kinderscout,/The cowdest place about".

Hope, etc: "Mony a mon lives in Hope as ne'er saw Castleton" (Old Derbyshire natives hate travelling even a couple of miles).

Killamarsh: "Let's make a Killamarsh fender" (a close ring of people round the fire).

Matlock: "It's like going round Matlock to get to Sheffield"; said by Chesterfield people of methods that are long and absurd.

Swarkestone Bridge: "He's driving his hogs over Swarston Bridge", which is narrow enough to squeeze the pigs and make them grunt, i.e. he is snoring.

Whaley Bridge: "It's Hell or Whaley, lad" (-do or die). Apparently connected with the High Peak Railway's short-lived passenger-carrying period, which ceased in 1877 after a fatal accident.

Outstanding are Derbyshire's comparisons. Here is a useful selection for your next conversation:

Fairly pleasant ones (unfortunately rather scarce): "Pretty as paint"; "It's near enough for t'thatch" (-as good as makes no difference); "as wick (-lively) as a maggot".

Unpleasant: "'E stinks like a foomart" (polecat); 'It's like ploughing with dogs" (working under enormous difficulties); "black as hell's delight"; " 'e's soft as cart grease/a brush"; "as wild as a woodland tup"; "'e's got a yed as big as a bucket!" (he's conceited); "It's like getting butter out of a dog's throat/giving donkeys strawberries" (-it's useless).

"Loving's in season when the gorse is in bloom" is said laughingly by lovers in South Derbyshire, because gorse there is rarely found without flowers. Finally two more sayings:

"As idle as Ludlam's dog (and he lay down to bark)".

"As throng (-busy) as Throp's wife (and she hanged herself with the dishclout)".

The second parts of these last two sayings may be omitted. Don't ask who Ludlam and Throp were: your guess is as good as anyone else's.

THE TEN COMMANDMENTS

ALL immigrants to the county, be they C. of E., R.C.'s, Methodists or any other fancy religion, are expected to embrace the Derbyshire one, enshrined as follows:

1. Tha mun speak reyt Durbyshire. This is t'fost an' t'biggest commandment.
2. Tha mun nivver speak B.B.C. Inklish nor owt instead o' Durbyshire.
3. Nivver coss an' swear — except when tha conna 'elp it.
4. Mark on t'calendar aw fairs, feasts an' well-dressins an' go to aw tha con.
5. Mind what yer dad an' mam says or yer'll cop it round t'ear-'ole.
6. Do nobody in — unless tha con ger away wi' it.
7. And not so much womanising either, specially if she's wed an' er owd mon knows thee.
8. Pinch nowt.
9. Speak the truth, the whole truth, an' ivverythink but the truth.
10. Dunna go on pinin' for thi neighbour's lawn-mower nor 'is best tablecloth nor colour telly nor owt what's 'is. When 'e's out, grab 'em.

N.B.—And if at church they let thee tek t' collection, mek sure tha puts it back.

ROUGH LANGUAGE

YOU WILL have to excuse certain expressions by your Derbyshire friends — they know no better. Often their language is indeed very blunt, as rugged as the ground they work on. A bad-tempered person is a *nazzy* ("nasty")—*britches,* a stubborn one is a *tup-eead,* a flatterer is a *slorm-pot* who *slorms* on you, a proud person is a *swank-pot,* and a *clack-fart* is a tell-tale. In occupations, a park attendant is a *snappy jack* and a chief organiser, man or woman, is *th'ead scrag.*

If you've rashly imbibed too much, you're *slottened;* if you're on such bad terms with someone that you're not speaking, then you *ave t' monk on.* If youanger a Derbyshire stalwart in any way, you'll meet threats like "I'll thrape ("hit") thee till tha's blathered i' blood", "I'll sluft yer", or "I'll clean out (or sometimes *pize*) thi lug-ole".

To judge by the descriptions given, Derbyshire is full of *looshers* ("slovenly women"), *ankle-biters* ("parasitic persons, spongers"), and *poor tools* or *not muchers* ("slow-witted people"). To these must be added the *proper sheenies* ("great cowards") and those who just stare vacantly at you, the *gongoozlers* who keep *gawpin'.*

The unkindest remarks are made to people who can't help their deformities. A *slip-jib* is someone with a receding chin. A cruel taunt to very round-shouldered people, and quite common in engineering works round Dronfield, was "I see you've brought yer kid wi' yer" or "You've got a Charlie on yer back", the last doubtless from Charles Laughton in the film "Hunchback of Notre Dame." Have Derbyshire folk no compassion?

A *government job* or a *cock job* is the term for any job done at work in the firm's time that should be done at home. And, since using a hammer is often a rough and ready solution, it appears under many joking names such as *knocking stick, knockometer* or *Manchester screwdriver* as if only lunatics from Manchester would be so daft as to hammer to bits a delicate piece of machinery.

Many thoughtless pranks are played on students and newcomers to industry. They are sent on errands for non-existent things like a glass *'ommer* or one to strike balances with, a loose nut, a metric screwdriver, a sky hook or a tin of tartan paint. Another heartless dodge is to send a lad for a *long weight,* so that at the other end he is kept waiting. In Glossop on April Fool's Day apprentices and new errand boys were sent for a pint of pigeon's milk with a sealed note requesting that they be sent somewhere else.

This frank and often violent language isn't just the privilege of the male. One "little woman" will call her neighbour a *gabbletraps* ("chatterbox"), and warn her own children, "Stop slawmin' (-wiping) yer 'ands along t'wall or I'll jowl (-cram) yer 'eeads in t'copper".

Of course, many Derbyshire folk do look a bit odd and rough themselves. Some are *twinny-toed* or *pin-toed,* others with the opposite appearance are *splother-footed* or *duck-footed.* Moreover life itself, like the language, is rough. After a brawl one little chap explained that he had got two black eyes and would have been given another but had no room. He was no worse than the navvy whom pals were urging, "Come on, Jack, tha's beatin' 'im". "If Ah'm winnin'," gasped their hero, "Ah shouldna like to be this other chap".

Many lifelong natives just ask for what they get. "How many students have you?", the head of a Derbyshire technical college was asked. "About one in ten", he replied absentmindedly. And it is not just the men who make unfortunate mistakes. A Dronfield lady, asked by her driving examiner how many feet she would need to stop when travelling at 30 m.p.h., said, "Two of course — one for t'clutch and one for th'accelerator".

But — all credit to them — there is no disputing their capacity for rough work, work that normally brings out the roughest language. After a long walk Bert, for instance, was returning along a tow-path when a barge appeared. "Hey", he said to the man on the barge, "Wilt give us a lift for a mile or two?" "Aye", came the answer as Bert jumped onto the barge, "but tha'll 'ev to work thi passage". "Aw reet", agreed Bert, "What's mi fost job?" "Ger on th'bonk an' pull wi' th'orse". Another inmate of the county, starting work as a roadsweeper, was told by his foreman, "Here's a brush, there's t'road, now ger on wi' it". Several days afterwards the man's worried *missus* received a first-class letter which read, "Tell 'em to send me a new brush. Ah'm i' Newcastle now".

COAL-MINING LANGUAGE

THE illustrious gentlemen of the South Derbyshire mining fraternity have graciously supplied live samples of their lingo. Here is your first lesson :

Down the Pit.

GI 'IT SUM OMMER "Apply a modicum of persuasive pressure".

ENYA GOTYER SNAP, SORRY? "Do you possess your prepared luncheon, my friend?"

AZE A DEEZ "He is working on the day shift".

ODE YEROSSES "Let us pause a moment for consideraation".

PITBONKSAFIEYER "The colliery spoilheap is blazing".

Concessionary Coal.

NOTE BUTSLEK "A scarcity of lump coal".

TH'STUF WUNNERBON "This coal is very difficult to ignite".

LODERODE RAMMIL "The quality of this fuel is unsatisfactory".

BITTERORATE "Satisfactory".

BY-LEDDY, BONNT AFE WEEUP CHIMDY "Excellent!"

On the Highway.

OJER "Stop".

AR TOJER YO SHUDDER KEP WEEYERWOR "No right turn".

AYUP, WAY NEELY ITTA BUZZ "Slow down".

ORATE, EVVIT YERRONE RODE "Give way".

ARTHOTE AYWER GOOIN SEEM RODE, STIDDA-THAT . . . "One-way street".

GIZZA SHUV MON "My car has stalled. Can you please assist me?"

NOTE BUTTUMPS ANOLLERS "Undulating country-side".

Etiquette.

GIZZADRAG "Kindly permit me to inhale from your cigarette".

AR DUNNER NO WOT AY SAZE INNER "I am unable to appreciate his choice of spouse".

ODE BUGGRUPTHEER "That gentleman of our acquaintance".

Other Useful Phrases.

WEERN YABIN? "Where have you been?"

BAKKUDS FORRUDS "Vice versa".

AZE BACK AFOOER AZE BIN ONNYWEER "His absence was not prolonged".

S'ORATE F'SUMMONYER "Just call me Jack".

WOMMIT "Depart for your place of residence".

WYE DUNCHER SEE WOT Y'MAIN "Kindly endeavour to be more explicit".

Students of grammar and phonetics will observe from this glossary that mining (like farming) clings very much to older ways of speech. Outstanding above are these features:

1. An *a* before *m* or *n* turning into *o,* as in OMMER ("hammer") and BONK ("pit-bank"). A North-West Midland feature well-known in Lancashire and Cheshire.

2. Survival of the sound *ay* for *ee* as in DEEZ ("days"). Still also used occasionally in Staffordshire and mid- and south Cheshire.

3. An occasional verbal plural in *-n,* which goes back to the Middle Ages. Compare above WEERN YABIN?, literally "Where have-n you been?"

Now you are ready to disguise yourself as a Derbyshire coal-miner, go down on the *cotton* ("winding-rope") and start hacking away. Perhaps you'll be lucky and find yourself on a *bull week,* a hard-working and well-paid week before a holiday when you pull out all the stops to get as much *dobber* or *knobs,* i.e. overtime, as possible. With oil and petrol the prices they are, you're badly needed.

FOOD AND DRINK

SOMETIMES *th'owd woman* will take a recipe out of a cookery book — quite right, it should never have been in it. For the man of the house to leave a *saucy plate* with food still left on it is the worst possible rebuff to her pride. The more usual snag, however, is to find ways of filling him. The typical *mester* often complains bitterly about being *proper clammed* ("very hungry") and is so fond of his *snap* ("food") that he goes to great lengths to obtain it. Give him half a chance, and he'll *guttle* ("guzzle") and *gollop* ("gobble") to his heart's content. At running buffets he steals up unnoticed for seconds and thirds, and lines his pockets with grease-proof paper to take plenty home for a good supper. The only trouble at such *do's* is that normal actions like smacking your lips and *swilkerin'* from your teacup into the saucer are frowned upon; and so is *dunkin',* dipping a hard biscuit into your tea. You can't even *grawnch yer grinders* ("crunch your double teeth") as you can comfortably at home.

If the Derbyshire *mon* turned his home into a cafe, this would be a traditional menu :

frumerty (wheat grains soaked and boiled, rather like porridge)
butties (slices of bread and butter)
peys ("peas")
collops o' bacon with no *sword* ("rind")
dog in a blanket ("roly-poly pudding")

Even after wallowing through all that, a true Derbyshirite would say, "I'm still clammed. I'll clean up t'devartials ("left-overs").

HOTELS, INNS AND PUBS

THE MOST FAMOUS Derbyshire hostelry is *The Cat and the Fiddle,* at 1,690 ft. among the highest in England. Although various explanations for the name have been suggested (e.g. from Caton de Fidele, governor of the English-held town of Calais in the Middle Ages), the most likely one is just that it is a whimsical nursery rhyme title given by the builder or a purchaser.

Derbyshire pub and hotel names glow with their own poetry. Splendid names like *The International Hotel, The Europa Hotel* and *The Palace* rise above humbler ones such as the various *Nags' Heads.* Some, such as *The Sitwell Arms, The Bold Rodney Hotel,* the many *Sir John Warrens* and even *The Blue Boy* and *The Green Man,* seem to commemorate people. Furness Vale's *Soldier Dick,* which stands for Richard Cromwell, Oliver's son, is associated with a local ghost. Care is needed too at *The Manners* and *Hurt Arms,* but all should be in your favour at *The Three Horseshoes* and *The Wanted.*

Sport looms large at *The Baseball Hotel;* food at two *Shoulders of Mutton, The Grapes* and two imported *Cheshire Cheeses;* and various strong liquids at *The Jug and Glass.* Most surprisingly, although Derbyshire is so landlocked, maritime influence comes out in *The Navigation Inn,* and two *Anchor Inns,* one of them out at sea at Tideswell. Occupations appear in *The Boot and Shoe, The Wheatsheaf* and all the *Railway Hotels.*

Derbyshire pub-goers seem very attracted to birds (feathered kind), for at opening time they approach every conceivable variety — *Bullfinch, Eagle, Grouse & Claret, Peacock, Nightingale, Robin, Woodpecker, etc.,* and even *Cock* and *Penguin.* Of four-footed animals, their special pets include *The Spotted Horse, The Waltzing Weasel,* and all the *Bulls' Heads* and *Red Lions.* The *Greyhounds* are a puzzle. Findern's is better known by its nickname *The Dirty Dog,* from which the nearby railway bridge is called

"He's been at the Buxton pump watter again".

Dog Bridge. Chapel-en-le-Frith has *The Black Greyhound,* looking like a contradiction in colours such as a green blackbird or a red bluebell. A third Greyhound, that at Carsington, is more famous as *The Knock* from the nearby place Knockerdown.

Don't be foxed by the signboards. Bradley's *Fox & Hounds* is really The *Jinglers,* and Littleover's *White Swan* is more properly *T'Mucky Duck.* And don't be startled by anything that goes on in such establishments. In one of them a customer staggered towards the bar and in so doing tripped over his pal who was prostrate on the floor. "Whiskey!" he gasped. "What about him?" asked the landlord, noticing the man on the floor. "Oh, he doesn't want any," was the reply, "He's drivin'."

A DURBYSHIRE DIKSHONERY

IF you can't find a Derbyshire word in an ordinary dictionary, that just proves it's not a *gradely* dictionary. Yet ignorance of spelling is a universal handicap. An Army storeman born near Ashbourne was handing out gardening tools. As each set was being taken, he had to list the items. Thus, when one recruit drew out a spade, he laboriously wrote *speed* and opposite it the figure "1". Unfortunately the next soldier had been sent for a scythe. After making several vain attempts to write this word, the storeman said, "Draw a shovel instead".

However, to help the situation we started compiling a dictionary the other way round, with Standard English words explained in Standard Derbyshire. Here is a section under letter A :

ADDLED "Rotten", of eggs without chickens or yeds without brains.

ADHESION. What meks a *cow-clap* stick to your foot.

ADJOURN. To knock off for a bit.

ADORABLE "Worthy of deep regard". Your *missus,* when you were *walkin' 'er out.*

ADULTERY. What *childer* grow up into.

ADVANCES. (1) What a young lad meks to his lass; (2) Any money you get on tick.

ADVERSARY. 'im you fell out wi'.

ADVERSITY "Trouble, misfortune". Like falling down a cellar grid.

The snag about making this dictionary was that good extra words appeared so thick and fast, prompted by rate demands, car smashes and so on, that before we had finished letter C we had to start all over again.

THE MEDIA

BASICALLY it seems curious that an area with such a strong identity should be receiving signals from all sorts of places and possibly be losing out in television coverage. Buxton, for example, receives A.T.V. Midland as well as Granada. But radio provides a service more tailored to local needs, in the highly efficient and popular programmes of Radio Derby.

As for the printed word, every issue of *Derbyshire Life* shows us another intriguing and wide-ranging view of county affairs, while local newspapers help to their utmost. Not only are they packed with information about the local scene, but they perhaps give a better interpretation of our national life than some of the more sensational national newspapers. Manchester's *Evening News* and Sheffield's *Star* keep trying desperately to civilise the Peaklanders, and within the county itself you are well served. Derby's *Evening Telegraph* keeps a vigilant eye on things, ably helped by a dozen weeklies from *The Derbyshire Times* to *The Buxton Advertiser* with its tireless columnist Fred Fletcher, and all excellent value. A quick reader from mid-Derbyshire can digest his *Deely Meel,* fascinating though it usually is, in about five minutes; but not his local paper. This doesn't mean that Derbyshire folk consider their local papers perfect. After his wife died, Sam thought he had better be in fashion and have the sad event noted in black and white. Calling at the news office, he asked, "How much dust charge?" "£3 an inch", was the reply. "Good heavens", exclaimed Sam, "She were over six foot tall!"

Why, here's a member of the mass media trying to contact you now.

WEATHER FORECAST

'ERE, owd on a bit. This is Radio Durbyshire. Ah've got some noos for thee. Fost thing it were too gleamy ("suspiciously bright") and then it began to mizzle ("drizzle"). Now it's foggy: yer conna see yerrandin fruntonyer. There's a cowd front movin' in from Russia in th'east, an' it aint arf gonner sile down — yer'll get a reyt dousin'. Up on Kinder it'll be starvin' ("very cold") wi' flaws ("heavy snowflakes"), woss nor owt we've 'ed this back-end ("autumn"). Last neet t'moon were pointin' down'ards, so yer con be sure it'll tip t'rain out. There wunna be much wind, so yer'll see smoke potherin' ("billowing") about. Keep t'cat in toneet, put on yer topcoat, shut aw dooers an' winders, an' stoke up yon fire till it goes reyt up t'chimdi. Outlook: 'Orrable. Still parky ("freezing") and mawky ("overcast").

CURES

CURES, or reputed cures, are legion. If you are stung by a bee or mauled by a lion, if you sprain your neck or break it, never fear because Derbyshire may hold an instant cure. Here follows a selection of genuine "remedies". Some are medically proven; others wait patiently for proof:

Ailment	**Cure**
warts	(1) Put egg water or eggshell on them. (2) Tie knots in a rush according to the number of warts. Touch each wart with a separate knot. Bury the rush in the soil and as it decays the warts will go.
sleep-walking	Wet a strip of carpet beside your bed. The chill will waken you.
children's bed-wetting	Make them eat stewed mice (also thought good food for people with no teeth).
chin-cough ("whooping cough")	(1) Roast a mouse and serve it unknown to the child. If the mouse doesn't cure the cough, it must be a fraud. (2) Drink from Bar Brook near Curbar.

other coughs	Goosegrease on brown paper clamped to your chest.
burns or scalds	Apply a plaster of fresh *cow-muck.*
skin disease	Sprinkle with gunpowder steeped in hot water.
hay fever	Snuff *sawt* ("salt").
back ache	Apply oil of juniper or a lump of sugar.
painful wounds	Put burning coal on a shovel and hold the wounded part in the smoke.
broken heart	Cover spine with a mustard plaster on brown paper and wrap the patient completely in blankets.

If you think some of these methods quaint and nauseating, compare them with older ones. To cure jaundice, for example, countrymen used to pour boiling water into a jar of common tar and, after it had settled, drink as much as possible of the water. If that prescription failed, a more revolting one was for nine nights to drink one's own urine, boiled in a saucepan immediately after midnight. Toothache, Derbyshire people used to believe, was caused by a little worm gradually gnawing a hole in the tooth. To combat this, they mixed powdered herbs and water in a container, dropped in a live coal and inhaled the smoke as long as they could bear. After this they breathed hard into a fresh glass or cup containing water, hoping the worm would drop out and be seen there. Clearly, with occasional aid from the National Health Service, Derbyshire remedies are becoming more reasonable.

Unhappily there is no cure for death. A dying man saw ham sandwiches on the sideboard and wanted one. "That's for t'funeral", was the blunt reply, "Thee get on wi' thi dyin'." Neither is there a cure for ingrained stupidity. Two Ilkeston men on a fishing holiday in Cornwall were wondering whether to put a cross on their boat to mark the place where they had hauled in a good catch. However, realising that next time they might have to go out in another boat, they left instead a newspaper on the water. Even the best logic course can't cure actions like that.

CUSTOMS

WELL-KNOWN at Marsh Lane, Ashford-in-the-Water, Tissington and many other villages are the annual well-dressings. Till the end of the last war, half Derbyshire villages relied wholly or partly on springs or wells as they had done for centuries past, so it is not surprising that the well has been a focus of village life.

Bakewell has perhaps the county's nicest one-day show. The local festival goes under several names, e.g. *Chawsath* ("Charlesworth") and *Bamford Wakes, Yawlgry* ("Youlgreave") *Feast,* and *Sutton Club, Fete* or (its oldest name) *Wakes.* Coal Aston on its *Feast Day* has had its custom (revived by the local school) of the *Bid-bid,* presumably meaning "Ask", where people ran round the village in a long line, holding hands and seizing anyone met.

In matrimonial customs, a startling though luckily rare one was to sell one's wife. A farmer Thomas Bott is recorded as having sold his to a man from Langley Common for 18 pence, signing a contract and delivering her up in Derby Market Place with a halter round her waist before several witnesses. For about a hundred years runaway couples could marry in the tiny parish church of Peak Forest. This useful custom was ended by Act of Parliament in July 1804, perhaps unnecessarily because elopers had then learnt that Gretna Green and Lamberton Bar near Berwick offered better facilities.

A long-established Shrovetide custom is that of football at Ashbourne with 100 or so players a side, an elaborately painted ball, and duckings and rough mauls in the Henmore Brook, which is part of the playing pitch. The Romans are alleged to have started this game, using human skulls. The games have been started by a long line of famous people, including in 1928 the Duke of Windsor, then Prince of Wales. The Duke also patronised the races on Flagg

Moor, and in the pavilion offered Woodbines to all around him. In this local sport there were originally 42 stone walls, but so many coping stones were knocked off that the course had to be altered and *fleeks* ("hurdles") used instead.

Plays include that of St. George, performed by groups of *guisers* or mummers at Christmastime and thought by many students of folklore to be a survival of an ancient mystery play. However, the most famous local play is undoubtedly the *Derbyshire Ram* or *Derbyshire Tup.* Characters, which include a farmer and other local worthies, mime the village butcher's slaughter of the legendary tup of famous qualities, no easy operation when the tup becomes restive. Relevant parts of the famous song "As I was going to Derby, sir . . ." are sung, usually as the acting proceeds. Where the entertainment began is lost in antiquity, but it is at least as old as the time when sheep rearing was a major British industry. It was an annual feature of Christmas entertainment in the mining villages round Eckington.

Many villages recognise Hallowe'en as *mischief night,* when under cover of darkness gates are removed from hinges, doors are securely fastened from the outside, etc. A Bradwell farmer, it is stated, watching several youths trundling a cart down Smalldale to dump it in the brook, decided to join in the fun, till he realised it was his own cart. "Hey, steady on. Stop, lads!" he remonstrated, but too late : his cart was heaved into the stream.

With measuring customs you need two special warnings. The first is that *tidy* and *nice* are units of measure. Thus *a tidy way* is a long way, and the comment, "There's a nice lot o' moggies in t'cellars", indicates an army of mice, however pleasant or not they are. Secondly, you must at all costs stand firm against continental measures. Otherwise Kinder Scout, majestic at over 2,000 feet, will shrink to a miserable 630 or so metres; and rugged Mam Tor to a pathetic 510. Write to your M.P. and do all you can to stop this tragedy.

Some customs are frankly no use. What about the Staveley chap who took the wringer upstairs to paint it because that's where the paint was? Or his pal, asked why he was taking a somewhat curious walk, who defended himself, "T'missus is away and t'dog's lost, so I'm tekkin t'wheel-barrer". Most local customs, however, are very useful. A farmer was asked whether he didn't find the steep approach to his hill farm inconvenient. "Nay", he answered, "When I've bought cows at auction at Bakewell Market, if ony of 'em coughs afore it reaches t'shippon, I awlus knows it's best to tek it back next week an' sell it quick".

BELIEFS AND LEGENDS

DERBYSHIRE is full of local history and legend. It harbours the *barghast,* a mischievous mountain spirit of Celtic origin, heard of mostly in the Peak District and corresponding to Lancashire's *boggart.* The word is probably German, although T. Wright's *Provincial Dictionary* claims it means "bar-guest!". The *wiffle-waffle,* the sound and action of sharpening a scythe, figures in a Derbyshire legend about a farmer who outwitted the devil in a mowing match. The loser was the first to *wiffle-waffle,* and that was the devil because the farmer had carefully stuck pins into the piece of ground the devil had to mow. On Baslow Edge is the Eagle Stone, a hard rock 25 to 30 feet high standing alone on top of the moor. Legend has it that Baslow lads had to climb it to prove their manhood.

In case you think the age of weird beliefs has long since gone, here is a modern one from *Swod* ("Swadlincote"). When an ambulance passes by, children chant, "Touch yer collar/Never swaller/Never catch yer fever". They hold their breaths as long as possible, believing this is how to escape infection.

Chesterfield's famous spire was, according to some people, deliberately erected with a twist. The story runs that the church authorities insisted in their contract that the church should be built "with a tower and spire", having themselves secretly inserted in the contract the last two words. The builder, realising the contract did not state what kind of spire, made a twisted one and so "twisted" them.

Derbyshire has so many mine shafts (about 7,000 according to one estimate) that it's surprising most natives haven't disappeared down them. Since the lead mines have been worked for over 1,800 years, it's no wonder they attract many beliefs. *T'owd mon* ("the old man"), besides being applied especially to abandoned mines and their waste material, stood also for the spirit of the mine. On Christmas Eve, miners used to leave half a candle burning in the mine for *t'owd mon* after they had finished work for the holiday. If you whistled underground, you were told off for "whistling the lead away". Another unusual belief was in the *knocker,* a mysterious tapping which many miners swore they heard. They thought that, if they worked in the direction of the noise, they would discover a rich vein.

A few Derbyshire optimists believe that money comes more easily than it really does. A Buxton quarry-owner would not raise his employees' pay. "Well", they said, "How about the same pay but more often?". In these inflationary times, there may be some sense in that. Another stalwart of the shire put a turnstile on his *chimdy-pot* at Christmas. A third argued with his section head, "Now look here; I've been working here five years now, doing three men's work for one man's pay. Don't you think it's time I had a rise?" "Tell me the other two chaps' names", said his superior, "and I'll sack 'em!" A fourth, told by his landlord that he was going to raise the rent, was delighted, saying how lucky it was because he couldn't possibly raise it himself.

Seriously, though, some beliefs are amazing. A few years ago the local press reported that, in Buxton and other places in the High Peak, a rumour had got around that a pig had upset a pram and eaten a baby. This story was denied by the police as "macabre and without foundation", but the rumour persisted. How credulous some good folk are!

CHILDER

DERBYSHIRE *childer* behave much like children the world over. Some are *mardies* ("spoilt children") or *mardy-soft* ("very spoilt") and do a lot of crying, which erupts in several stages. They usually start by *gernin'* ("groaning"), change to *skrikin'* or *yellin'* ("screeching"), and end up *beh-alin'* ("bawling") or *'owlin'*. The most troublesome, insistent ones are *wherrets.*

But many youngsters are of a sturdier breed, relishing games whose names and rules have been handed down through the years. It is Derbyshire veterans who best remember these games, though. They were brought up before the days of the all-embracing *telly,* when you were lucky if you had a battery-powered *wireless* and had to use your imagination, imitating cowboys and Indians seen in matinees of silent films, perhaps at Heanor Empire or Ilkeston's Kings. Tuppence downstairs, wishing Saturday morning would never end! Ah, what bliss!

There was a definite cycle of games throughout the year. Spring saw the gay spinning of tops and the trundling of hoops along the road (killed by the dangers of modern traffic). This was followed by skipping, hopscotch, *snobs* (called *firestones* in other parts), *fag cards* against the walls of school playgrounds, and *tick.* Then came the time for marbles, of which only the *glassies* seem to survive. Where are all the *dobbers, blood-alleys, tenners* and *twentiers* hidden? With autumn would come the horse-chestnuts, called *conkers* in civilised Sheffield but *cob-jaws* or *cobblers* in Chesterfield and district. A *cobbler 3,* for example, would be one that had broken three rivals. Boys used to toughen their *cobblers* by leaving them all night in the oven or keeping them a long time before playing with them. Then finally, as the nights lengthened, there would be miming games under the flickering street lamps and wild chasing games in winter.

This didn't exhaust the inventiveness of Derbyshire's *childer.* There was *swig-stick,* rather like hockey, with knob and ball; and *trip-cat* or *dog-stick,* where a stone, etc., jerked from a balanced piece of wood had to be hit as it fell. A great favourite was *husky-fusky* or *rusticabum,* called in other counties *Spanish leapfrog.* Another was *tin-a-lurky,* where a lad (or lass) stood with one foot on an old tin can while the rest of the gang raced away to hide. When the tin's guardian came to search for you up *snickets* and in tiny front gardens, you had to rush out, race him back to the tin and kick it down the street, with a triumphant yell of *Lurky!* In the *holler* game, your searcher reminded you all, "If you dunna holler, I shanna foller." You would then hide and try to distort your voices by shouting into your cupped hands — this was *hollerin'.* When found, you would race back to the *den* to see who was *on* next time.

Bull-roaring, as heard, e.g., around Grindleford, Langwith and Whitwell, was caused by stuffing a drainpipe with brown paper and lighting it (paper, not drainpipe) so that it made a sound just like the roaring of a bull. This was usually done on dark nights by a crowd of children who scattered when the roaring began. Another game can well be imagined from the pidgin-English rhyme that accompanied it : "Me no know/Me no tell/Me press button/Run like hell (or *Ring a bell)".* Another game that irritated householders, especially on *Mischief Night,* was *knick-knacking.* This needed a button, pin and length of cotton pulled from a distance to cause a mysterious window-tapping. And there was *bunny running,* chasing opponents from house to house via gardens, fences and hedges. What a lot of first-hand excitement is missed by those brought up only on monopoly or "Match of the Day!"

THE DERBYSHIRE RAILWAYMON

THIS FELLOW is a very different breed from his brothers in other parts of England. He used to work for the old L.M.S., which he called "Th' 'Ell of a Mess" or "Lord's My Shepherd" or "Let Me Sleep"; or perhaps for the *Knotty,* a term still used for the old North Staffordshire

"I on'y want to send 'em to Sheffield — not buy the flamin' train".

line to Crewe via Stoke. These names were for contrast with other poorer railways that he would talk about, such as the "Late and Never Early" (L.N.E.R.), "Languisher and Yawner" (Lancashire & Yorkshire Railway), "Slow and Dirty" (Somerset & Dorset Railway), and the "Go when Ready" or ironically "God's Wonderful Railway" (G.W.R.).

Fortunately, although our railways have been nationalised, his speech has not, and his railway terms often differ widely from those elsewhere in Britain. What other localities called *fluff* ("porters' tips") is to him a *weasel,* and if you want to tip him you have to *weasel* him. A ground signal for proceeding on a branch line, a signal often called *pig's ear* or *lunar lights,* is at Derby *feathers;* another type known elsewhere as a *domino* signal is to him *cat's eyes;*

and a distant signal usually called *bull's eyes* or *back boards* is to him *back 'uns* or *back pegs.* Likewise occupations seem to change, so that the *snip, shark* or *scud* of other areas ("ticket collector" to you) is Derbyshire's *ticket snapper.*

For a derailment there are many terms, e.g. "We're on t'floor/in t'dirt/in t'soft soil/we've 'ed a pile-up", this last generally referring to a collision. Similarly for a ground signal there are different layers of language. One man will say, "You've got t'dummy (or *dolly*) off", whilst another, speaking more "refaned", will state, "You've got the dwarf signal".

Many words have been lost. Most train names have disappeared with their trains; but *Tutbury Jinnie,* the passenger train between Tutbury and Burton-on-Trent, is remembered. There are no more *banjos* ("shovels") simply because there are no more firemen; and if you asked on your commuter journey for a *lilac wonder* you would be thought a little mad, because these purple day-return tickets are now extinct.

In railway parlance, places acquire unusual names. *Weetabix Junction* is Burton Latimer because the original Weetabix factory was sited near a former junction there. British Rail Divisional H.Q. at Nottingham is called despairingly *The Kremlin.* The Severn Tunnel and indeed any tunnel is *The Hole.* In signalmen's talk *passing the Cross* refers to Clay Cross, *The Mills* is Clay Mills, and *The Gate* is of course Ambergate.

Railway language at Derby keeps being modernised. The *refresh* is the refreshment room; the *bowling green* is the fast line which, with its enormously long metal sections, does seem beautifully smooth; and an *Abadan* is a driver who uses too much oil. *Tin cans,* so-called from their shapes, are 32-ton hopper coal waggons feeding *merry-go-round* power stations, where trains go in carrying coal and then leave to return to the colliery. These *tin cans* are opened and closed by lineside pedestals called *Darlics* after those in the children's T.V. serial.

Did you know that Derbyshire train speeds used to depend on the days of the week? Normally it was better to go at 20 m.p.h. rather than 40 because of longer hours and higher pay; but on Friday, which was pay day, engines were *in Friday gear* to get their crews home quickly.

The language of workers from overseas brings problems, not least on the railway. One of our coloured cousins objected to being told off, saying, "You only pick on me because I'm a nigger"; another objected to being told that red and yellow buffers needed cleaning "because they become black after a while"; and a Pakistani interpreted the famous set of words in British Rail regulations about "after the hours of darkness, in fog or in falling snow" as "when it becomes daylight . . ." That's logical really!

Equally logical is a certain Derby train driver. Knowing that time is all-important on the railway, he bought from an auction an alarm clock, but it started losing 40 minutes an hour. One morning he woke up, looked at the clock and went back to sleep, to be awakened by the rattling of milk bottles and the milkman asking, "Dust want ony extra toneet?" It was 4.10 p.m. Angrily he kicked the offending clock round the bedroom till to save his toes his *missus* threw it into the dustbin. Now he's invested in a brand-new clock but keeps it an hour fast so that, as he says, "It doesna seem then as if I'm gettin' up so early".

A DERBYSHIRE QUIZ (answers on Page 32)

1. (a) Where is Stonyshire?
   (b) Which is The Cathedral of the Peak?
2. Which is taller, the spire of Ashbourne Church or the tower of Derby Cathedral?
3. What was Derbyshire's lowest cricket score — 16, 26 or 36? And the highest — 645, 745 or 1645?
4. (a) What are these Derbyshire animals? — a nuzzock (also called a *Nazareth* or *moke);* a rot; a mowdy.
   (b) Name these birds and insects — throstle; spink; 'Arry-long-legs; battle-twig.
5. Is the Murder Stone (a) an obstruction in the bowels, (b) a sacrificial stone at Arbor Low, (c) a wayside

memorial to a murdered man, (d) Unstone?

6. Which Derbyshire towns, villages or great houses appear in fiction under these names? — (a) Amberdale, (b) Lambton, (c) Morton, (d) Snowfield, (e) Pemberley?
7. Are *bachelor, embore* and *wibbet* (a) notes of a primitive local music, (b) personal nicknames, (c) measurements of different sizes of roof slate?
8. If you've missed your *cale,* have you missed (a) your turn, or (b) a vegetable?
9. Was the Snake Pass named from (a) its winding nature, (b) its treacherous character, (c) the crest of the Devonshire family, who owned the Snake Inn?
10. Where can these bizarre book titles be found? — "Cursory Remarks on Swearing", "Boyle on Steam", "Haughty-Cultural Remarks on London Pride", "D. Cline on Consumption."
11. What rivers run through these dales and valleys? — (a) Beresford, (b) Chee, (c) Darley, (d) Hope, (e) Woodlands.
12. Is a *strickler* (a) a member of a religious sect, (b) a flat piece of wood to crush lead ore, (c) a nickname for boys tickling trout in Derbyshire rivers?
13. Is Little John's grave at (a) Littleover, (b) Hathersage, or (c) Hayfield?
14. Is the Cat Stone (a) near the Cat & Fiddle, (b) on Stanton Moor, (c) just outside Derby?
15. How are Darby and Joan connected with Derbyshire?
16. Who was proclaimed King of England in Ashbourne market place, yet never came to the throne? — (a) The Black Prince, (b) Brian Clough, (c) Bonnie Prince Charlie?
17. Where did the local fire brigade, attempting a demonstration, mistakenly set alight a newly tarred road? — (a) Foolow, (b) Great Hucklow, (c) Repton.
18. Are the Gospel Hillocks (a) the site of an old Derbyshire monastery, (b) pre-historic tumuli near Flagg, (c) mineral spoil-heaps from the Ranter Mine?
19. What distinguished personage had glass cylinders

specially made and brought to Derbyshire in trying to grow straight cucumbers? — (a) Lord George-Brown, (b) George Stephenson, the railway pioneer, (c) George IV.

20. Arrange these people in order of importance — (a) t'mester, (b) t'missus (sometimes very curiously called *our folks*), (c) our kid, (d) mi marrer or mi butty.

ANSWERS TO QUIZ

1. (a) Derbyshire, in George Eliot's *Adam Bede;* (b) Tideswell Church.
2. The same (212 ft.).
3. 16 versus Notts. in 1879, and 645 versus Hants. in 1898. With luck, this season both records may be improved upon.
4. (a) donkey, rat and mole; (b) thrush, chaffinch, daddy-long-legs and earwig.
5. (c), on the Whaley Bridge-Disley road, recording the murder of William Wood, an Eyam weaver.
6. (a) Ambergate, in D. H. Lawrence's *Virgin and the Gipsy;* (b) Bakewell, in Jane Austen's *Pride and Prejudice;* (c) Hathersage, in Charlotte Bronte's *Jane Eyre;* (d) Wirksworth, in George Eliot's *Adam Bede;* (e) Chatsworth, in *Pride and Prejudice.*
7. (c). 8. (a). 9. (c).
10. In Chatsworth Library. They are dummy book titles painted on the backs of doors to make shelves look continuous.
11. (a) Dove; (b) Wye; (c) Derwent; (d) Doe and Peakshole Water; (e) Ashop.
12. (b). 13. (b). 14. (b).
15. Only, it seems, through the county's Darby and Joan clubs. The fictitious names come from a 1735 poem in *The Gentleman's Magazine.*
16. (c). 17. (b). 18. (b). 19. (b).
20. The terms mean (a) husband or father; (b) my wife; (c) our child or my brother/sister; (d) my workmate. But you had better decide their order or importance or heaven help you!